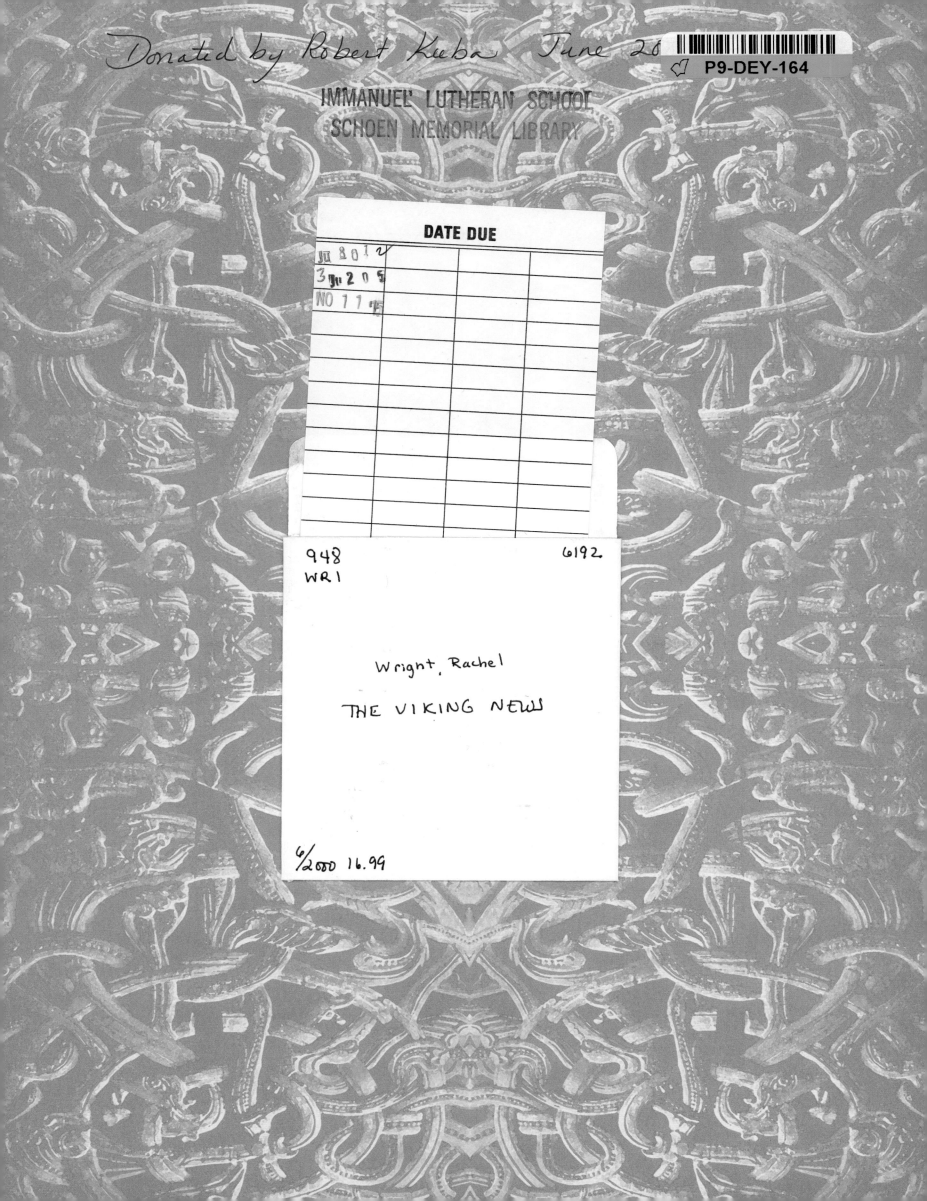

DATE DUE

JU 8 0 1 2			
3 JU 2 0 5			
NO 1 1 05			

THE VIKING NEWS

AUTHOR: RACHEL WRIGHT ✦ CONSULTANT: RICHARD HALL

DEAR READER,

You know how much we Vikings love to remember brave deeds and valiant heroes. Well, now it's the turn of *The Viking News* to follow in this tradition, by celebrating our finest achievements in this special edition of our great newspaper.

We've included stories about our most famous kings, most daring explorations, and most fearless raids. But that's not all! We also bring you fascinating articles on the many unique features of our way of life — from how to throw a fantastic feast to how to prepare yourself for battle.

Read and enjoy!

Rachel Wright

CHIEF RUNE-MASTER!

A NOTE FROM OUR PUBLISHER

Of course, as we all know, the Vikings didn't have newspapers.
But if they had, we're sure that *The Viking News* would have been the one
everybody was reading! We hope you enjoy reading it, too.

Candlewick Press

CANDLEWICK PRESS
CAMBRIDGE, MASSACHUSETTS

CONTENTS

MAP OF VIKING SETTLEMENTS

GREENLAND

Atlantic Ocean

ICELAND
Thingvellir

NORWAY

SWEDEN

FINLAND

RUSSIA

Shetland Islands

Lindisfarne

Århus

IRELAND

DENMARK

ENGLAND

Stamford Bridge

Dnieper River

EUROPE

Paris

FRANCE

Black Sea

Luni
Pisa
Rome
Constantinople

SPAIN

ITALY

Strait of Gibraltar

Mediterranean Sea

NORTH AFRICA

Legend:
- VIKING HOMELANDS
- AREAS VIKINGS SETTLED
- ▲ VIKING TRADING CENTERS IN OTHER LANDS
- ➚ VIKING RAIDING ROUTES

Map by GILLIAN TYLER

OUR RAID PAYS OFF!

Illustrated by CHRIS MOLAN

SMASH AND GRAB: Viking raiders pull off a daring raid at the island monastery on Lindisfarne.

TODAY, IN 1066, we Vikings are feared throughout Europe for our fast and furious raids. Yet 300 years ago, few people had heard of us. Here, *The Viking News* looks back to the key event that made us headline news.

ON JUNE 8, 793, a small group of Vikings landed their ships on Lindisfarne, a remote and desolate island just off the eastern coast of England.

On Lindisfarne was one of the most famous Christian monasteries in the world. But the Viking visitors were not there to worship! Instead, they stormed right up to the monastery, killing any monks who barred their way. They seized as many riches as possible, then raced back to their ships and sailed away, before anyone could catch them.

This attack stunned all of Europe. Until then, we Vikings had made very little impact on our neighbors. But that was about to change!

In the past, we had mostly stayed in our homelands of Norway, Denmark, and Sweden, fishing, working on our farms, and often fighting amongst ourselves.

But we'd also had some trading contact with the outside world and had noticed the wealth of other lands just across the sea.

Even in those days, we Vikings were the finest shipbuilders and sailors in all of Europe. We had swift ships capable of crossing the stormiest seas, as well as the skills needed to sail them.

So it was only a matter of time before we used those skills to try and get some of that foreign wealth for ourselves.

Lindisfarne's treasures and its isolated position made it the perfect target.

And what a success that first raid was! Not only did it strike fear in all neighboring lands, it showed other Vikings how easily wealth could be taken from abroad.

Hundreds of other raids quickly followed. Our great Viking Age had begun!

VIKING TRIUMPHS

Illustrated by GEOFF HUNT

THROUGHOUT the 800s, the pages of *The Viking News* were crammed with reports of daring raids and bold deeds. Here are three of our favorite stories from this exciting time.

BLOOD BRIBE!

NEWS FLASH! March 845: For the first time ever, our raiders have been offered a fortune just to leave their victims in peace!

WORD HAS just come in of yet another triumph for our warriors abroad.

A large fleet of Danish ships sailed up the Seine River into France and looted the city of Paris.

Anxious to stop the raiders from advancing any farther, the French king has agreed to pay them a staggering 3,000 bags of silver — if they will simply go away!

Never before have we been bribed to do nothing! Easy money like this makes raiding a more tempting idea than ever!

SWEDISH STUNNER

NEWS HAS REACHED US that a huge Viking force is attacking Constantinople — one of the world's greatest cities! A reporter from *The Viking News* is at the scene.

THIS DAY, June 18, 860, will long be remembered. I am standing on board a ship on the Black Sea, watching as a Swedish fleet lays siege to the vast city of Constantinople — the capital of the mighty Byzantine Empire!

Already our men have raided the coastline near the city. And now, as the attackers' ships draw in close to the city walls, every Viking raises his sword up high, as if to shout, "Prepare to die!"

Few would dream of launching a raid on the most powerful city in Europe, but this feat is nothing to us Vikings!

This isn't the first time we've sailed the Dnieper River to the Black Sea.

For many years now, our traders have grown rich exploring Russia and even trading with far Constantinople itself.

But as today's assault shows, our warriors will forget trade if they think they can get wealth and glory by force instead.

And not even the greatest city in Europe can stop us!

STOP THE PRESS!
A sudden storm has scattered the Viking ships and prevented them from capturing Constantinople. But this show of strength proves to the world that we're a force to be reckoned with!

THEY FEAR NO ONE: Viking raiders approach the great city of Constantinople.

REACH NEW PEAK

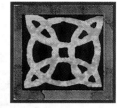

OUR UNSTOPPABLE RAIDERS!

SEA OF BLOOD: Danish raiders battle their way through an enemy ambush in the Strait of Gibraltar.

AFTER THREE LONG years abroad, Danish leader Bjorn Ironside is back at last from the longest raiding trip yet known. Here, he tells *The Viking News* his amazing story.

IT ALL BEGAN back in 859, when my old friend Hastein and I assembled a fleet of 62 ships and set out from our raiding bases in northern France. Our aim was gold and glory, and we were willing to go a long way to get it!

We began with a few quick raids on the west coast of France and then headed on to Spain.

We lost two of our ships off the coast there, but in return got a fine haul of gold, silver, and slaves. And once we'd gotten through the Strait of Gibraltar, the entire Mediterranean Sea lay helpless before us!

We were unstoppable, raiding along the coasts of Africa and southern Spain, until all our ships were groaning under the sheer weight of the loot and slaves they held.

But still we carried on. We wanted our voyage to be remembered forever!

Our next plan was to go to Italy and attack the famous city of Rome. But when we got to the coast of Italy, we lost our way completely, and ended up sacking just the cities of Pisa and Luni instead!

By now, we had been away for long enough, so we set out for home. But our greatest challenge was still to come. When we sailed into the Strait of Gibraltar, we found a fleet of ships from Spain waiting. And the men on board had a score to settle.

It was an epic battle! The sea turned red with blood, and many brave Vikings were lost. But Hastein and I fought our way out with 20 ships and sailed back to France.

MISSION ACCOMPLISHED!

And now our adventure is over. These last three years have left us rich beyond belief. But better still, our names will be famous forever.

What true Viking could ask for more? ▨

EXIT TO ICELAND

TO THE

Illustrated by PETER DENNIS

PILLAR OF FATE: Ingolf solemnly lowers a wooden pillar into the sea.

BETWEEN THE YEARS 982 and 1001, a Viking father and son both explored farther west than any European had ever dared. And by discovering two new lands, they astonished the Viking world.

TODAY, ICELAND is an important part of the Viking world. But until 870, it was just an empty wasteland. Here, *The Viking News* remembers the very first settlers who brought about this change.

IT WAS THE Norwegian brothers Hjörleif and Ingolf Arnarson who first set sail to colonize Iceland — a mysterious land that few people had ever visited.

They risked death in doing so, for it would be a long and dangerous voyage. But if there was the chance of finding good farmland there, it was a risk worth taking.

The brothers packed their families, followers, and slaves into just two boats, along with all their animals and supplies.

The difficult voyage took several weeks, and many times the boats were nearly sunk by storms. But at long last, Iceland came into sight.

Then, Ingolf took two wooden pillars from his carved ancestral chair and lowered them into the gray sea. Wherever they washed ashore, he said, would become the settlers' new home.

For two years, Ingolf roamed the coast in search of the pillars. At last, they were spotted in southwest Iceland. They had come ashore in a beautiful bay, where hot springs flowed through a green and fertile land.

The settlers' courage and patience had been rewarded — they had found enough land for many families to share.

Since then, almost 35,000 Vikings have started new lives in Iceland. What better tribute could there be to the bravery of those first few settlers?

VIKING EXPLORERS need to be tough, and no one was tougher than Erik the Red. His great voyages began in 982, when he was exiled from Iceland for three years for killing two men in a feud.

Erik promptly picked a crew and went to sea in search of an unexplored land that was rumored to lie west of Iceland.

A WORLD OF ICE AND SNOW

Erik and his crew sailed the Atlantic Ocean until at last they saw the land they sought. Its east coast was entirely icebound and uninviting, so they sailed on along the coast. And there, on the south-west shores, they found ice-free land with plenty of good green pastures.

Three years later, Erik came back to Iceland, bursting with tales about the marvelous place he called Greenland.

By that time, Iceland was becoming crowded, and farmland was scarce, so Erik's stories appealed to many. In 986, some 25 ships left for Greenland under Erik's command.

It was a dangerous voyage, and only 14 ships made it safely to the new land. But two settlements were founded that have flourished ever since.

But that wasn't the end of the explorations. In the same year, a man named Bjarni Herjolfsson sighted

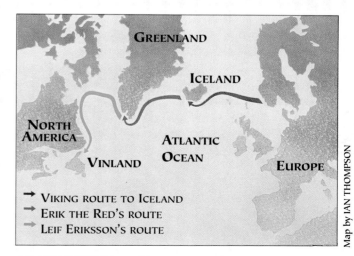

ISLAND HOPPING: Viking routes to the west.

EDGE OF THE WORLD!

Illustrated by GEOFF HUNT

EDGE OF THE UNKNOWN: Leif Eriksson's ship sails past lonely forested shores on the way to Vinland.

a new landmass, which was even farther west than Greenland.

No one was more excited by Bjarni's story than Erik's son, Leif. And, determined to match his father's achievement, Leif set out in 1000 in search of the mysterious land.

Leif Eriksson sailed west until he reached a rocky, barren shore. He then headed south, past a forested coast, until he found a land that was richly fertile.

When he returned to Greenland in 1001, Leif described his discovery to *The Viking News* and explained why he had called the land Vinland.

"There were lots of vines, laden with berries called grapes," he said.

"I hadn't seen wild grapes before, but one of my slaves is from Germany, where grapes grow, and he knew what they were."

Leif's expedition was soon followed by others, all eager to bring home Vinland's vast supplies of timber, grapes, and fur.

Some hardy folk also tried to settle in Vinland, but it proved to be one Viking colony too many.

What Leif didn't know

when he found Vinland was that people were already living there. Soon, fights between locals and settlers grew so fierce that the Vikings had to leave.

A PLACE TOO FAR FROM HOME

One dejected settler told *The Viking News* that the colony could never have survived. "It's too far from Greenland," she said, "and

far from essential supplies of tools and weapons."

Despite this setback, however, *The Viking News* salutes the achievements of Erik and Leif. Between them, they have unlocked the mysteries of the far western seas and the unknown lands beyond.

And in so doing, they have proved again that we Vikings are the greatest explorers in the western world! ◪

OUR GREATEST KING

Illustrated by DAVID BROWNE

IT TAKES COURAGE, luck, and ruthlessness to rule over any Viking land successfully. Yet Cnut, our greatest ruler, reigned over all three — and England too! We take a look at his action-packed career.

WHEN CNUT first made the headlines, during his father Svein Forkbeard's conquest of England, in 1013, we at *The Viking News* knew that he was a man worth watching. A born leader, Cnut came from a very long line of formidable Danish kings.

A MAN OF METTLE

Cnut soon showed us his strength of character, when his father died, early in 1014. Still only 18 years old, Cnut now had to take command of his father's armies and deal with a strong English counter-attack.

We cheered for our young champion through the many tough battles that followed, and even more when, in 1018, Cnut was finally proclaimed king of all England.

In the following year, Cnut's elder brother died and Cnut succeeded him as king of Denmark. Clearly, here was a leader who meant business.

Cnut spent the next 10 years strengthening his rule over England and Denmark. But we knew the list of his triumphs would not stop there, and we were soon proved right.

Norway and Sweden, who had been enemies, now ganged up to invade Denmark. Without delay, Cnut went on the attack.

He gathered such an impressive fleet that as he sailed to Norway, the enemy fled before him. Cnut was able to seize control without fighting a single battle! Now Cnut ruled Denmark, Norway, and part of Sweden, as well as England. This was an incredible feat.

Cnut ruled well and is remembered as a wise and just king. He made sure all his followers stayed on his side by visiting them regularly and exchanging gifts. For seven years, his lands were at peace.

But with Cnut's death, in 1035, the good times ended. None of his sons was able to keep control of so many countries, and soon all the Viking homelands fell back to fighting one another.

Cnut had ruled over us wisely and well — but sadly his day was gone. We will not see his kind again.

KING OF ALL HE SURVEYS: Cnut, on a royal tour, visits one of his English earls.

A HERO FALLS: Harald lies dead — along with Viking hopes of future greatness.

THE LAST VIKING?

Illustrated by CHRISTIAN HOOK

ON SEPTEMBER 25, in this year of 1066, Harald Hardrada, the king of Norway, was killed while trying to reconquer England. A reporter from *The Viking News* was there and sent this account of how Harald's death may mark the end of Viking power.

I AM CROUCHING down behind my shield on the battlefield of Stamford Bridge, near the English city of York. Around me lie the dead and dying of King Harald's army.

Since Cnut's death, no other Viking ruler has attempted to win back England. But this army seemed to have a strong chance of success, for its leader was Harald Hardrada — a hero in the finest Viking tradition.

His skill and daring in fighting at home and abroad were legendary. So too was his reputation as a brilliant commander, a generous friend, and a fearsome enemy. In fact, few Vikings have ever had a career as glorious as King Harald's.

But now his hopes of conquest lie in ruins. And as I hide here, watching his defeated warriors flee back to their ships, I can't help wondering whether we shall ever see a hero like Harald again.

But this terrible defeat means more than the tragic loss of a great king. It's also a reminder of how hard it is now for our men to gain wealth by attacking other lands.

Back in the days of the Lindisfarne raid, the lands we plundered were badly led. But now they have strong kings, who control many lesser lords and all their fighting men. That is how the English king was quickly able to raise the powerful army that defeated Harald today.

MORE TRADE, LESS GREED

And that's not all. Many of our people have now settled in England, Ireland, and France, and trade between our lands and these has grown. We are more closely tied to the rest of Europe than ever before, and so we are less free to attack it.

In short, times have changed. We may soon find that Harald's defeat today is not just the end of a great leader, but also the end of the mighty raids that have terrified Europe for 300 years.

Although Harald's memory will live on in our hearts forever, the greatest triumphs of our people may well be in the past.

BIGGEST THING ON

Illustrated by PETER VISSCHER

OPEN-AIR MEETINGS, or Things, are regularly held across the Viking world. But for sheer size and spectacle, nothing compares with the great Althing of Iceland, as this Icelandic farmer explains.

FOR ME — and for many people in Iceland — the Althing is the highlight of the year. For starters, it means two whole weeks without work!

ALL THINGS TO ALL MEN

Every summer, we leave our farms behind and travel to the great plain of Thingvellir, in the southwest of Iceland.

Here we gather at the base of a mighty cliff to hear the Law Speaker recite our laws — and to agree on new ones. And we discuss important issues that affect Iceland.

It's also the place to patch up any feuds that have developed over the year and to punish those people found guilty of serious crimes.

Of course, in all parts of the Viking world, men from every community meet at Things to discuss their local matters. But our great Althing stands alone. None of those other Things can match it for one simple reason — its huge size.

Thousands of people from the *whole country* come together here. And because of this, it gives us a unique sense of belonging to a single, united Icelandic nation.

But as well as all the

HEART OF A NATION: People from all over Iceland gather at Thingvellir for the Althing.

politics, the Althing has unbeatable entertainment to offer too — it has the biggest fair in Iceland!

Rows of booths and tents stretch right across

the plain, almost as far as the eye can see. People roam everywhere — there are traders and travelers bringing news from far-off lands, men competing

in trials of strength, and brewers pouring out beer to keep everyone merry.

And not only that, if you're looking for love, this is the place to be!

DOES CRIME PAY?

MURDER: A man is slain in cold blood.

NOT EVERYONE thinks the Althing is perfect, however. *The Viking News* reprints this letter we received from an outraged victim of crime.

THREE MONTHS ago, my neighbor attacked me after a quarrel. He

was taken before the Althing and ordered to pay me a lot of money as

compensation. But has the scoundrel paid up? Has he, my helmet!

The problem is that the Althing hasn't got the power to make sure its rulings are carried out. Many villains just ignore

its orders — and this always leads to trouble!

Last year my friend was murdered, and his killer was banished from Iceland by the Althing.

But because no one could force him to leave,

EARTH!

CLASS TEST

FROM KING TO slave, every Viking plays a part in making our lands prosper. But how much do *you* know about other people's responsibilities? Try this special lifestyle quiz to find out.

There is one *incorrect* answer to each section. See if you can find all four.

1 As a KING you should:

a) Defend your country successfully.
b) Conquer other lands whenever possible.
c) Set a good example by saving money and living simply.
d) Gain a reputation for great generosity by giving gold arm rings to your followers.

2 As an EARL you should:

a) Rule over a district of many farms and households.
b) Provide your king with men and ships in times of war.
c) Make local freemen pay you the highest taxes they can.
d) Give as much help and advice as possible to the freemen in your local district.
e) Spend time learning social skills, such as playing the lyre and reading runes.

3 As a FREEMAN you should:

a) Compete with your neighbors for the best land available.
b) Make sure your land will supply you with enough to eat.
c) Pay taxes to your local earl in return for his protection and help.
d) Join up willingly if your local earl calls you to fight.

4 As a SLAVE you should:

a) Work for a king, earl, or freeman and follow your master's orders at all times.
b) Remain loyal to your master in the hopes that one day he may grant you your freedom.
c) Accept that you can never go to a Thing.
d) Take no more than two weeks of vacation in a year.

ANSWERS

1c: A king defends his country and attacks other lands to get wealth. To do this he needs the best men available. So he must attract them to his court by lavishing them with gold and good living. If not, he'll soon lose power.

2c: A great earl is expected to behave like a mini-king — ruling his district and helping out his king *and* freemen. If he sets his taxes too high, he'll get no help in times of trouble or war.

3a: Any freeman — be he a tradesman, farmer, or merchant — relies on good relations with all his neighbors, as well as with his local earl. It helps having friends close by in times of need.

4d: Are you serious? A slave's life is work. If he gets two *days* of rest a year, he's lucky!

Many men bring their sons and daughters here, in the hopes of making good marriages to the children of rich land-owning families.

All in all, you can see why the Althing is a truly great event. So come next year! If you don't, you'll miss out on one of the best Things in life! ▨

---

the scoundrel stayed in Iceland. So my friend's family took revenge by burning down the killer's house — with him inside.

Now both families are at each other's throats in a blood feud that will run for years. This must stop! It's high time the Althing forced criminals to pay their dues. ▨

REVENGE: The killer's house is burned to the ground.

FIGHTING FIT

Illustrated by CHRISTIAN HOOK

OUR POWERFUL LONGSHIPS are without a doubt the finest fighting ships in all of Europe! Here a master boatbuilder tells *The Viking News* just what makes them so special.

1 The first thing any ship needs is a strong keel — it's the backbone that supports everything else.

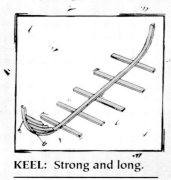

KEEL: Strong and long.

For a longship's keel, I will use only the very best-quality oak, which I cut from the trunk of a single straight tree.

2 The next thing is the hull, and it's the hull's unique shape that makes the longship so formidable.

The base of the hull should be made as flat as possible. This is why our longships can sail in far shallower waters

HULL: Flat and light.

than other warships — allowing our warriors to raid almost any town near a coast or river.

Each plank of the hull is cut as thinly as possible. This makes the longship incredibly light, which means, of course, that it's also stunningly fast — nothing can beat it for speed!

3 Once the hull is in place, the deck is laid, using strong, close-fitting planks.

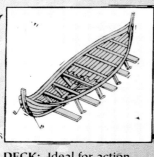

DECK: Ideal for action.

Longships are built for fighting, so the deck is kept free of anything that might get in the crew's way. Many of our longships don't even have benches for the rowers to sit on. Instead, they make do

with the wooden chests used for storing their weapons and armor.

4 After this, the mast is added. Like the keel, it is fashioned from a single tree trunk.

MAST: Easy to take down.

The mast must be tall enough to support the huge sail, and yet have the strength to withstand the fiercest ocean gale.

It must also be easily raised and lowered so

that the crew can switch from sail to oar at a moment's notice — vital for a quick getaway when the wind's in the wrong direction.

5 Our longships are envied throughout Europe, and rightly so! But even the finest ship is worthless without a good crew.

People fear our ships because of the warriors who sail them. Viking men are fine sailors, powerful oarsmen, and bold fighters — it is they who make our ships so deadly. ▨

SHIP FACTS

Sizes of longships vary greatly, but most are between 60 feet and 90 feet in length. The larger ships can carry more than 50 warriors at a time.

Despite their large size, many longships are still actually light enough to be dragged out of the water and pushed on rollers for short distances overland. This is essential when rivers are blocked by rocks, rapids, or waterfalls.

Many longships can reach the formidable speed of 17 miles per hour in a strong wind. Even when under oar, the maximum speed is still amazingly fast — 7 miles per hour.

The biggest and most famous longship of its day was built in 998 by Olaf Tryggvason, king of Norway. Named *The Long Serpent*, it was a staggering 121 feet long and was powered by the strength of more than 68 rowers!

BJORN'S BATTLE TIPS

Illustrated by CHRIS COLLINGWOOD

OVER THE YEARS, hundreds of young lads have prepared for battle by reading Bjorn Bloodaxe's advice column. Here's just a small selection of the many problems he's solved concerning Viking warfare.

⊡ My mate says that a Viking's main weapon is his sword, but I say it's his ax. Who's right?
Your mate is, of course, you numbskull! What are you thinking? Of course, an ax, a spear, and a shield are very useful weapons in battle. But a strong sharp double-edged sword is the most highly prized weapon a Viking can own.

⊡ How much should I spend on a sword?
Some lucky Vikings are given a good sword that's been in their family for generations. The rest of us should buy the best sword we can afford — you'll find it pays off when you go into battle.

⊡ Is it very important to decorate your sword hilt with gold and silver?
A fancy hilt is fine if you're rich and powerful and want everyone to know it. But at the end of the day, it's the quality of the blade that counts — a poorly made blade could easily break just when you need it most.

⊡ I've heard that the very best swords have pattern-welded blades. What does this mean?
A weaponsmith makes a pattern-welded blade by twisting several strips of iron together into a spiral, then hammering the spiral out flat and polishing it smooth.

Because of all the different strips inside it, the blade is unlikely to shatter when it hits something hard — such as your enemy's head!

ARMOR RATING

⊡ I can't afford a suit of chain mail. What should I wear instead?
If you can't afford chain mail — and let's face it, few of us can — opt for a padded leather tunic. It'll protect you from all but the fiercest blows.

As far as headgear goes, an iron helmet is ideal, but if your battle funds are limited, stick with the hard leather helmet you wear when practice fighting with your friends.

⊡ I'm eight years old and want to start using a proper weapon. Why won't my dad let me?
Because you're far too young, that's why! Be patient and work hard at practice fighting with blunt wooden weapons. Only when you start growing hair on your chin will it be time to use a real ax or sword.

⊡ Now that I'm 15 years old, I'm ready to win glory by fighting great battles overseas. Where do I start?
Slow down, son — first things first! Start by joining up with your local earl, to get some fighting experience and build up your reputation. Only then will you be ready to join a king or great earl on a full-scale expedition overseas.

But don't worry — good men are always needed, and if you're courageous, ruthless, and skillful, you'll make it before long!

MAN OF IRON: Bjorn Bloodaxe models the best in arms and armor.

GOING BERSERK

BERSERKS are the most terrifying of all warriors. But do these violent, half-mad men of war really help our armies? *The Viking News* asked two old warriors for their opinion.

FIRST WARRIOR

If you want to know why berserks are feared by all our foes, go and fight alongside them! The ones I knew would have scared away the fiercest giants!

Before a battle, they put on bearskin cloaks to gain the strength of a bear. Then they started working themselves into a frenzy of blood lust!

And when they rushed into battle in this state, they fought like mad dogs, hurling themselves at the enemy as if no sword could harm them.

Some people say that the berserks eat strange berries and that these cause their battle rage. Others say the madness runs in their families.

Whatever the truth, I can vouch for their power. When our foes saw them, they turned white and fled. Anyone who can do that to an enemy is all right by me.

HE'S GONE BERSERK AGAIN!

Cartoon by TONY KENYON

SECOND WARRIOR

Berserks are strong and terrifying warriors, I'll give you that. But the ones I fought beside were far too uncontrollable and unreliable for my liking.

You see, there was no telling what they might do when the fury came upon them. Sometimes they'd charge off into the enemy's midst and lead us into a trap.

And that's not all. I once knew a berserk who fought so furiously that he collapsed from exhaustion and dropped dead in the middle of a fight — without suffering a single wound!

I mean, if that isn't letting the team down, I don't know what is! ▨

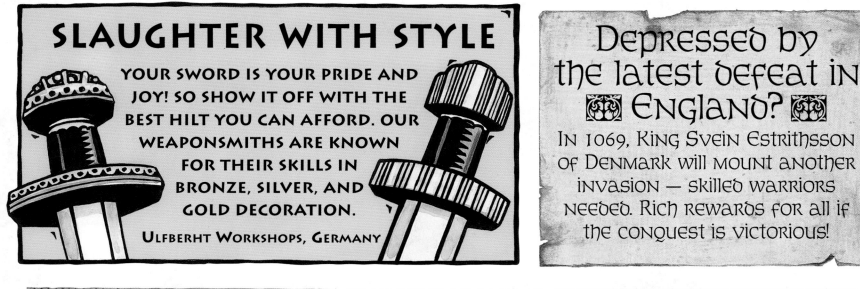

GOODS THAT OUR TRADERS WANT

FUR
from Russia

JET
from England

SILVER
from the East

SLAVES
from eastern Europe

Volga River

Dnieper River

WINE
from France

GLASS & CLOTH
from western Europe

Black Sea

Caspian Sea

SPICES
from Persia

Mediterranean Sea

SILK
from Constantinople

THEY KNOW NO BOUNDS

Illustrated by PETER VISSCHER

OVER THE YEARS, brave Vikings have made incredible journeys in order to trade in far-off lands. Here, we celebrate the achievements of Europe's greatest traders.

WE VIKINGS may be best known for raiding and exploring, but it's also no secret that we're first-class traders as well!

Many of our raiders are traders too, and once all the fighting finishes, they're the first to seek out profitable goods. As a result, there's no end to the foreign luxuries we now enjoy back home.

The markets of far-off Constantinople provide our warrior-traders with wondrous silken cloth, as well as spices and jewelry. And in exchange, our men leave valuable goods from the Viking lands, such as amber, soapstone, animal fur, and walrus ivory.

But if Constantinople offers massive rewards, getting to them is not an easy task. Our brave lads must first sail down the Dnieper River, in Russia, then cross the stormy Black Sea.

The Dnieper is full of treacherous rocks and rapids. And while some hardy traders manage to haul their boats around these dangers, many still come to a tragic end.

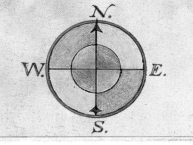

GOODS THAT OUR TRADERS TAKE ABROAD

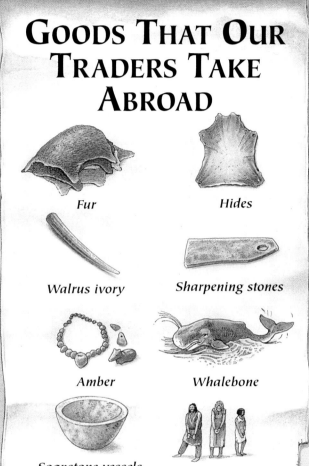

Fur

Hides

Walrus ivory

Sharpening stones

Amber

Whalebone

Soapstone vessels

Slaves

However, not much stands in the way of a profitable deal, and some traders have journeyed even farther to get rich.

EASTERN PROMISE

Today, most of our silver comes from mines in Germany, but this wasn't always the case. In the early 900s, groups of Swedish traders sailed hundreds of miles down the perilous Volga River to reach the shores of the distant Caspian Sea.

There they met with traders from lands in the mysterious East, who had both precious silver and fragrant oils to sell.

But wherever they go, our Viking traders take their skills as fighters and sailors with them.

Add to that their eye for a bargain, and it's no wonder our traders are second to none!

MEET THE MARKET

Illustrated by ANDREW WHEATCROFT

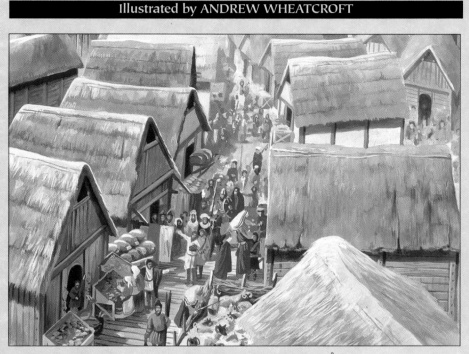

STREETS AHEAD: Trade flourishes in the bustling town of Århus.

TRADING TOWNS are rare, and many of us have never seen one. So our reporter took a trip to the bustling port of Århus, in east Denmark, to bring you this taste of what life in a market town is like.

PEOPLE everywhere! That's the first thing you notice when you enter Århus — it's often difficult even to move in the busiest streets.

Inside the defensive walls that surround the town, the streets are lined with the houses of craftsmen, such as blacksmiths and bone carvers, all busy selling their goods from stands in front of their homes. You'll see merchants here too — Vikings from Norway, Sweden, and Iceland and other traders from England and the rest of Europe.

Farmers from the local countryside come in to exchange their pork and beef for the supplies they need. And down at the wharf, the quays are packed with ships bringing in goods from countries all over Europe.

There are plenty of bargains to be had here — you might pick up a soapstone cooking cauldron from Norway, or a strong German grindstone to turn your grain to flour.

After the quiet of the country, the noise and bustle of Århus is often shocking. But the ceaseless shouting of the traders signals the success of the town.

And don't forget — it is in places like this that our traders and craftsmen increase the wealth of our lands.

KEEP THE GODS ALIVE

Illustrated by VANESSA CARD

IT'S NO SECRET THAT a new religion, Christianity, is sweeping across our lands and driving out our old gods. But not everyone is prepared to change the way he or she worships. We asked a traditional believer to explain why he won't become a Christian.

THOR
Strong, fierce, and a lover of food, Thor is the god of thunder. He uses his hammer to protect both gods and people from evil giants.

NJORD
God of the seas and the winds, Njord looks after those who travel or go fishing at sea. He is also god of money, trade, and possessions.

OF COURSE, I know that some people still believe in our Viking gods, but everywhere you look, Christianity is gaining the upper hand.

CHANGE FROM THE TOP

I blame our kings for this. Most of western Europe is Christian, and if our rulers want to be treated as equals by the foreign kings, they have to be Christian as well.

But when a king takes up Christianity, he wants his people to do the same. Soon Christian priests arrive, and the old ways are slowly lost. This is what happened in Denmark in the 970s. Norway was next,

and now Sweden is going the same way.

But why should we turn against our gods? Thumping Thor! They take good care of us.

If you want to marry, you call on Freyja, the goddess of love. For a good harvest, you pray to Freyr. Whatever you need, one of the gods will help you.

And the gods allow us to worship privately and in our own way. The most we have to do

is to sacrifice a dog or horse to them once in a while and sometimes go to outdoor festivals held near sacred lakes or forests. Usually we just pray to them in our own homes.

PRAYERS AT A PRICE

But now we're all being forced to build costly churches and attend organized services.

And Christian priests are telling us how and when to worship. That's just not Viking style.

No, I for one will never abandon the old gods. They've stood by me in the past — and I'm determined to stand by them now. ▨

ODIN
Odin is the mightiest of the gods. The god of war, poetry, and wisdom, Odin is powerful, treacherous, and skilled in magic. His horse, Sleipnir, has eight legs, and his two birds, named Thought and Memory, keep watch on the world for him.

FREYJA
Freyja is by far the most important goddess and looks after luck in love and fertility. She is also a goddess of war.

FREYR
The brother of Freyja, Freyr is one of the most powerful gods. He has control over crops and fertility and is also the god of wealth, health, peace, and nature.

BURIED IN STYLE

Illustrated by NICK HARRIS

ONE OF THE MANY changes that Christianity has brought about is the way that we bury our dead. Here, *The Viking News* mourns the passing of a glorious tradition.

MOST VIKING burials today follow the laws of Christianity. The body is placed in a wooden box or shroud and buried in sacred ground.

But it wasn't always this way. A hundred years or so ago, our burials were very different.

GO WELL PREPARED

In those days, we wouldn't have dreamed of burying our loved ones without putting some of their belongings beside them for use in the next world.

A man would expect to take a few tools or weapons with him, while a woman would want some pieces of jewelry and cooking equipment.

But today, Christianity forbids anyone to be buried with anything at all. And this rules out the greatest tradition of our noble Viking past — the spectacular ship burial.

Our ships have always been our most prized possessions, and it was common for people to be buried with model ships, or in boat-shaped graves. But some kings, queens, and earls went further — they were actually buried in real full-sized ships!

The boat would be set into a pit and laden with goods and riches. Often, the dead were joined by freshly killed animals, such as horses and dogs. And occasionally, even a slave was sacrificed, too, and laid inside the boat.

And when all these lavish preparations were finished, the ship was covered over with a mighty mound of dirt.

Such sights may be half forgotten now, but we should remember these great customs of our past with pride. ▨

FIT FOR A QUEEN: A treasure-laden ship awaits the body of a Viking queen.

IRON MAN IN TRAINING

Illustrated by MIKE WHITE

A BLACKSMITH'S SKILLS make him one of the most important people in any village. But as this young apprentice reveals, it is not an easy trade to learn.

I ALWAYS wanted to be like my father. He's the best blacksmith in our area and one of the most respected men around.

You name it, and he can make it — everything from pots and pans to knives, locks, and keys. And he repairs tools and weapons, too. In fact, the whole village would grind to a halt without him!

IT'S A DIRTY JOB!

Now that I'm 13, I'm old enough to learn the trade myself. And it's painful work, I can tell you!

I have to do all the nasty, dirty, unskilled jobs in the workshop. But at least I'm building up the strength I'll need for beating iron all day long.

I work the bellows for hours so that the fire stays red hot and heats the iron to the right temperature. And once my dad's hammered the

HOT STUFF: There's more to blacksmithing than bashing.

iron into shape, I fetch the water to cool it down.

But I can also watch my dad. He knows how hot the metal has to be before it can be shaped, and how to remove weak spots to make it strong.

It'll take years to learn it all. But one day I want to specialize in making high-quality weapons. Men pay a lot for a good sword, because their life depends on the skill with which it is made.

Who knows, maybe I'll end up working for an earl and become even richer than my dad! ▨

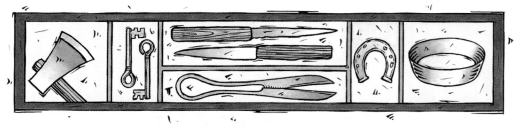

KNOW YOUR RUNES!

Illustrated by VANESSA CARD

F U TH O R K H N I A S T B M L Y E G

TERRIFIED BY RUNES? Unsure how to use them? Take heart — help is at hand! Here, *The Viking News* shows you the full runic alphabet and explains exactly how these marvelous letters can be used.

LET'S FACE IT, few of us can write. And since all our laws, history, and poetry are passed on by word of mouth, few of us need to, either!

But don't ignore our runes. This easy Viking alphabet is well worth learning. For starters, people will admire you for your unusual skill.

And because runes are made up mostly of simple straight lines, they are incredibly versatile, too. They can be carved into almost any surface!

WRITE ON!

With a good knife, you can write runes easily in wood or bone. This makes runes a great way of keeping your favorite things safe. Just carve your name on your bone jewelry box or wooden comb, and thieves will be less likely to steal them!

But runes have their finest use when carved into rock. By recording your achievements in solid stone, you keep your name alive forever. What better reason could there be for learning your runes today?

STONES FOR THE DEAD

YOU MAY NOT be able to raise dead loved ones from the grave, but you can leave a rune stone in their honor. Simply follow these four steps.

1 Look for a large flat rock in a place where plenty of people will see it. Choose the smoothest side to work on and carve a snake shape all around the edge of that side.

2 Carve a rune message inside the snake's body. Say something about the dead person's achievements, and record your own name, too. Paint the carvings red.

3 Now carve a picture or symbol inside the rune border. Choose an image from Viking art, such as an elaborate four-legged beast or a coiling dragon.

4 To finish, paint your carvings to make them stand out clearly. Red is good for pictures as well as runes, but brown, black, and blue are excellent, too.

A MATCH FOR OUR MEN!

Illustrated by CHRIS MOLAN

IN CONTROL: No rest for this farmer's wife, as she runs both home and farm while her husband is away.

MOST VIKING WOMEN stay at home while their menfolk are risking their lives abroad. But that doesn't mean that these women aren't pulling their weight, as this farmer's wife told *The Viking News*.

OUR FIGHTING men may get all the headlines, but believe me, women are just as important. If it weren't for the endless child rearing we wives do, there'd be no men to fight in the first place!

To see how vital we are, visit any freeman's farm. For starters, all farmers' wives have many domestic chores to do.

We have to prepare the food, take care of the children, and supervise milking the animals.

We must make all our family's clothes, too. And let me tell you, spinning the wool and weaving it into cloth takes a lot of

time, skill, and patience!

But that's not the half of it. For months every year, many men go off trading or fighting and leave us wives in charge of the farm.

We have to make all the vital decisions about what to sell and what to buy, when to gather in the harvest, and what to store up for the winter. And we must give orders to all the slaves as well.

It adds up to a big responsibility. And men know it, too! Compared to women in other parts of Europe, we Viking wives

are given a lot of respect.

For example, when we marry, we keep control of any wealth or property we bring with us as a dowry. In other countries, the husband takes it all.

DON'T MESS WITH US!

Not only that, if our husbands treat us badly, we're allowed to divorce them! This is very rare outside our Viking lands!

All we have to do is state our wish in front of a few witnesses and we're officially divorced!

When all's said and done, we Viking women can match our men in most departments. Some wives even go with their husbands on trade trips to foreign lands.

Other women have made risky journeys to settle abroad. A famous widow, Aud the Deep-minded, sailed to north-west Iceland and set up a colony there. It became an important settlement that grew to 80 farms!

With women like us as mothers and wives, it's no wonder our men are so tough!

CALLING ALL COOKS

Looking for the perfect cooking pot? Then try our soapstone cauldrons! They won't dent like metal or crack like pottery, and they're large enough to cook a family-filling stew!

Cuningsburh Carvers, Shetland Islands

LOOMS WITH VROOM!

Our sturdy wooden looms are perfect for making clothes. Just lean them against the wall and get to work! Make room for a loom!

GET WEAVING CARPENTERS, SKARA, SWEDEN

SMOOTH AS BONE

MAKE WRINKLED CLOTHES A PROBLEM OF THE PAST WITH ONE OF OUR WHALEBONE IRONING BOARDS. TO USE, SIMPLY STRETCH YOUR CLOTH ACROSS THE SMOOTH BOARD AND RUB IT HARD WITH THE GLASS BALL.

IRON IT OUT, BORRE, NORWAY

TAKE A TIP

Illustrated by MAXINE HAMIL

VIKING WOMEN ARE responsible for treating any illnesses that occur in their household. And over the years, the women readers of *The Viking News* have passed on countless fascinating remedies for others to try. Here, we reprint some of their best tips from the past.

HORSE POWER!

This classic method for stopping a wound from bleeding was sent in by a reader from Denmark.

Take a big handful of fresh horse dung and put it in the sun to dry. Rub it down into a fine powder, then put a thick layer of this powder onto a linen cloth. Leave the cloth wrapped around the sufferer's wound for a single night. This will stop the flow of blood.

MAGIC MEDICINE

A reader from Sweden recommends this vital precaution.

Prevention is better than cure, which is why I'm always telling people to

carry lucky charms to ward off illnesses. I've tried many charms in my time, but my favorite is a jackdaw's skull. I've kept it in my belt pouch for years now and never had so much as a cold!

BARKING BITES

A mad dog's bite can kill. But here's what a reader from England does to treat the poison.

Pick the leaves of the

two herbs agrimony and plantain. Mix them with some honey and an egg white and then apply the mixture to the bite. This is guaranteed to stop the wound from becoming badly infected.

TUMMY TROUBLES

A reader from Orkney sent in this messy, but useful, piece of advice.

Feeling queasy? Chances are that you're suffering from worms. To get rid of the pests, just swallow a few bracken or corn cockle seeds. Then sit back and wait. The seeds will flush the worms — and everything else for that matter — out of your system in no time!

COOKING QUESTIONS

Illustrated by EMILY HARE

WHEN IT COMES TO FOOD, we Vikings like things simple, hot, and filling. But that doesn't mean food preparation is always easy. Here we chew on the tough questions sent in by some of our hungriest readers.

❓ What's the best way to preserve meat and keep it from rotting?

In the fall, preserving meat is a vital skill. We just haven't got enough food to feed all our cows, pigs, and sheep over the long cold winter.

After slaughtering the animals, you can either hang the meat on a rack to dry in the open air, smoke it over a fire, or pack it away in salt. Any of these ways will keep meat good for months.

❓ My mother's stew tastes like boiled rope! How can I get her to make it less revolting?

Easy! Tell your mother that dried meat or fish must be cooked *slowly*, at a low heat, to bring out its full flavor.

Adding salt and herbs to the cauldron will also perk a stew up — and help disguise the taste of any

meat that may have gone bad! Try cress, coriander, dill, fennel, or celery.

❓ Why is my wife's bread so full of grit?

It's likely the sandstones she's using to grind her corn to flour. As she turns the handle to grind the grain between the two stones, tiny pieces of sandstone are getting mixed in with the grain!

The only way to spare your teeth is to buy lava-rock grindstones. They're

much more expensive, but they're harder, too, and won't chip so easily.

❓ I love wild berries and pick lots of them in the summer. How can I preserve them all winter long?

This method works for any fruit you might pick, including plums, apples, or cherries. Preserve your fruit either by drying it in the sun, or by covering it with honey. Guess which way's better for Vikings with a sweet tooth! ▨

BEER — SHEER POETRY!

IT'S WELL known that we Vikings drink far more beer than any other kind of liquid — and that includes water! To celebrate this, *The Viking News* prints this poem by the talented winner of our famous Beer Is the Best! poetry competition.

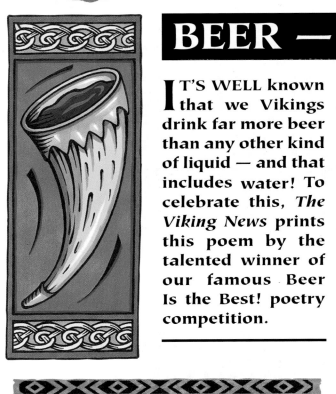

Bring me a drink to give strength to the bold
And to spur on the boy in the fight.
Bring me a drink that will comfort the old
And care for the sick in the night.
But bring me no milk to pour in my horn,
Nor water, ice cold from the spring.
And what use is juice on a sharp frosty morn?
I need BEER to make my heart sing!

✦

Its dark bitter barley taste touches my tongue.
I drink to the sound of the song I have sung.

Superb! A vat of beer to our winner!
(And a mug of water for our runners-up!)

DICING WITH DEATH

Illustrated by CHRIS MOLAN

THE GIANT KILLERS: Norwegian hunters close in on a mighty whale.

WE ALL STRUGGLE to raise enough animals and crops to survive on. But some people have to go to dangerous lengths to feed their families, as these three men told *The Viking News.*

FIRST HUNTER

I live in north Norway, where there's not much good land for farming. As a result, whales, seals, and walrus are our main sources of meat.

It's really quite easy to hunt seals and walrus. Basically, we just wait for them to come ashore, and we either shoot them with an arrow, or skewer them with our spears.

Whales, on the other hand, are a very different matter! You have to use boats to herd them into shallow water, where they can't swim properly, and then stab them with spears. It's not a job for the faint-hearted, since a large whale can easily smash a boat with one flick of its tail!

It's worth the risk, though, because whales are profitable catches. We eat their meat, carve their bones into strong, lightweight tools, and use their oil to fuel lanterns.

Walrus are nearly as useful. Whenever I bag a couple, I skin them, then twist the skins into ropes to sell at the local market. Their strong ivory tusks are ideal for carving, too.

SECOND HUNTER

Whale hunting is child's play when compared with killing caribou! I live in west Greenland, where these huge reindeer are our main source of meat.

The best way to hunt caribou is to use dogs to drive them into a dead end, where your friends can ambush them with spears and arrows.

But you need to keep your wits about you. Just one false move and the stampeding caribou could trample you to bits under their hooves!

THIRD HUNTER

Well, if you think whale or caribou hunting is dangerous, all I can say is think again!

I live in the Shetland Islands, where sea birds, such as gulls, kittiwakes, guillemots, and puffins, lay their eggs in the cliffs high above the water. We often climb these cliffs to collect the eggs in baskets and to net the birds for their oily meat.

And let me tell you, climbing a treacherous, crumbling cliff, with only a rope to steady you against a cold, whipping wind, isn't a job everyone would jump at!

REACH FOR THE TOP: It takes nerves of steel to hunt sea birds and their eggs.

STAND OUT IN STYLE

Illustrated by SUE SHIELDS

EYE-CATCHER: It only takes a little effort to look stylish.

ATTENTION, all Viking men! Are your looks getting you down? Our fashion editor, Helga Finelegs, tells you how to dress to impress.

CLOTHES

It's a fact that everyone, from kings to freemen, wears the same basic clothes — an undershirt, a tunic, trousers, and a winter cloak. So if you want to be noticed, it's vital to make your clothes stand out in a crowd.

A lot depends on the quality of the cloth. Most men can't afford to buy imported luxuries, such as silk, but homemade cloth can go a long way if it's carefully woven.

Your undershirt must be made of linen and your cloak either of wool or fur. And don't forget — your tunic and trousers must always be woven from the finest wool. The coarser the threads are, the poorer you'll look!

Everyone can make clothes colorful by using vegetable dyes, but there are other tricks to try, too.

A decorative border makes a lot of difference to an outfit. Strips of colored linen, wool, or even silk can be twisted into patterns and sewn onto your clothes.

Another good tip is to have designs embroidered onto your tunic. If you're rich, you could even have gold and silver threads woven in with them.

JEWELRY

Silver or gold rings for your fingers, arms, or neck are a good idea, as they are clear signs of wealth. And since you'll need a brooch or pin to fasten your cloak, why not invest in an ornate one, gilded with silver?

BEARDS

A beard should always be trim and tidy — not like an overgrown bush! But remember, it doesn't matter how beautifully your beard is shaped if it's crawling with lice and nits. So comb your hair regularly — we women don't like beards that are alive with bugs!

PERFECT PINAFORES!

Illustrated by SUE SHIELDS

TIMELESS STYLE: The classic elegance of the pinafore.

LADIES, IT'S TIME to celebrate an all-time classic of Viking style! Here, Helga Finelegs explains why she thinks pinafores are still the best.

VIKING WOMEN are just not as stylish as they used to be!

These days it seems as though every woman in northern Europe is wearing the same long, loose dress style. It may be fashionable, but it's also boring!

I think it's time to take a tip from the past. Back in the mid-900s, we Viking women had a wonderful style that was uniquely our own.

The key to it was the pinafore dress. Made of soft wool or linen, it hung straight down at the front and back of the body, from two shoulder straps.

The pinafore's sides could be sewn up, to give a slim and elegant look, or left hanging open, for striding about the farm.

Of course, the pinafore wasn't worn on its own. That would have been both immodest and cold! So a long shift of wool or linen went underneath.

The final stroke of fashion brilliance was the pair of oval brooches used to attach the shoulder straps at the front.

These brooches were both stylish and practical.

Not only did they hold up the pinafore, but long strings of gorgeous glass, jet, or amber beads could be hung between them.

The women who could afford them wore finely decorated silver or gold brooches. But there were plenty of simpler bronze brooches, too.

It's true that women today do still wear other Viking classics. Cloaks are still fastened with a three-pronged brooch. And long hair, knotted at the back of the head, is still the preferred style.

But nothing replaces the pinafore-and-brooch look. It was truly Viking fashion's finest hour. ▨

FEASTS FANTASTIC

Illustrated by NICK HARRIS

THROWING A FEAST may make you popular, but there's a lot more to it than simply serving food and drink. We asked an earl's wife to give us the lowdown on how to make it all run smoothly.

❓ Firstly, who should you invite to a party?

Well, if you're an earl or a rich freeman, hosting a feast is perfect to impress important neighbors. It also helps spread a lot of good will.

So my first invitations always go to the nearest earls and their wives. Then I invite the more important freemen, who pay my husband taxes in return for his protection.

❓ When is the best time to hold the feast?

To really impress all your guests, hold it at a time of year when food supplies are running low, such as late winter.

To pull this off, you'll have to plan well ahead and preserve lots of extra food when supplies are more plentiful.

You'll need more than you think — people stay on for days after a good party! And try to stow away a few surprises, like rare German wine. Your guests won't forget that!

❓ Is it critical to have an entertainer?

Oh, absolutely! If you haven't got anyone on your farm who can play the lyre and tell some poems, you'll just have to employ a traveling story-teller instead. He may cost you a few silver coins, but if he keeps the guests amused and keeps them from remembering old arguments they've had, he'll be worth it!

❓ Can there be trouble at a feast?

Guest unrest *can* be a problem. Most earls and rich freemen will bring their sons and closest followers with them. So before you send out the invitations, check that no one from your household has ever offended any of these extra guests. You don't want fights starting!

It's safest to insist that weapons are left outside the feasting hall. And tell your warriors to keep watch and not get drunk. It has been known for someone with a grudge to wait till a party was in full swing, and then burn the house down.

We all love a warm party atmosphere, but no one likes it that hot! ❖

PARTY ON: Invite a storyteller to your feast and you'll cook up a sizzling atmosphere.

THE BATTLE BEGINS!

Illustrated by IAN THOMPSON

WE ALL LOVE to play the board game Hnefatafl, but we often argue about the rules. To prevent any more fights from breaking out, *The Viking News* presents the official rules, as compiled by our games reporter.

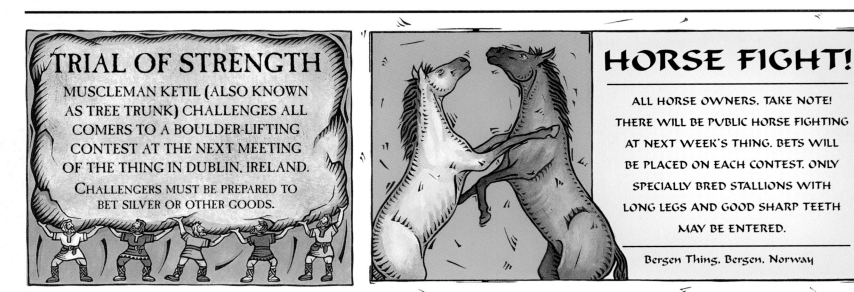

PREPARATION

⚙ Hnefatafl is a game of strategy for two players. Each player has an army of warriors and tries to out-think his or her opponent.

⚙ First, decide who will control each army. The red army consists of 12 warriors and one king, while the white army has 24 warriors but no king.

⚙ Set up the board as shown on the left, with the red king on the middle square and his red warriors defending him. The white warriors sit around the edge.

THE AIM OF THE GAME

⚙ The white player's aim is to capture the red king.

⚙ The red player's aim is to move the king safely to *any* square at the edge of the board.

HOW TO MOVE

⚙ The white player starts.

⚙ The players take turns moving one piece.

⚙ All pieces can move across, up, or down, but they are NOT allowed to move diagonally.

⚙ All pieces can move *any number of spaces* in one direction — but they cannot jump over the top of another piece.

⚙ Only the king can sit on the center square.

CAPTURING A WARRIOR

⚙ A player can capture an enemy warrior by trapping it between two of his or her pieces (see picture below). The red king is the only piece NOT caught in this way.

⚙ If a piece is captured, it is taken off the board.

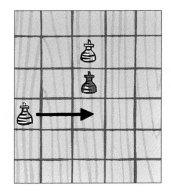

Important!
If a player deliberately moves one of his or her own warriors between two enemy pieces, it is NOT captured by them.

CAPTURING THE KING

⚙ If the king becomes surrounded by four white warriors (see the picture below), he is captured.

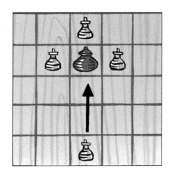

WINNING THE GAME

⚙ If the king is captured, the white player wins.

⚙ If the king manages to get to any square at the edge of the board, he is safe, and the red player wins the game.

◆ A PERFECT FAMILY HOME! ◆

WARM AND COZY FARMHOUSE NOW AVAILABLE IN ICELAND.

Consists of one main living room for cooking, eating, and sleeping. Features include traditional central fireplace and wall benches that double up as beds.

Made of wind-proof turf blocks on a stone base; it has wood-lined walls to keep out the cold and damp.

Conveniently situated on good pastureland, close to a clean spring.

A bargain for any young farmer!

APPLY IN PERSON TO:
ODD STURLSSON,
REYKJAVIK, ICELAND

TOWNHOUSE FOR SALE

oven   straw thatch

toilet   path   living room   workshop

SMALL NEWLY BUILT HOUSE IN LUND, SWEDEN — IDEAL FOR A CRAFTSMAN AND HIS FAMILY.

❖

THE HOUSE, WHICH WILL LAST FOR AT LEAST 15 YEARS, BOASTS A SPACIOUS WORKSHOP, IN ADDITION TO A LARGE LIVING ROOM. ITS WALLS ARE MADE FROM INTERWOVEN BRANCHES COVERED WITH CLAY, AND ARE GUARANTEED DRAFT PROOF. READY FOR VIEWING NOW. IT MIGHT BE THE BUY OF YOUR LIFE!

❖

APPLY TO BOX NO. 3058

LAND SALE!

Small fenced plots of good-quality land are now on sale in a village in Denmark.

Each plot has great potential as a cattle pen, crop field, or as a site for new farm buildings.

Apply in person to:
THE BIG FARM,
VORBASSE, DENMARK

PUBLIC NOTICE

✦

THE KING OF DENMARK REMINDS ALL TOWN DWELLERS TO KEEP AN EYE ON THEIR LAMPS AND FIRES AT ALL TIMES. CLOSELY PACKED WOODEN TOWNHOUSES ARE VERY VULNERABLE TO FIRE. BEWARE!

✦ **By the** A.D. 700s
The people of Denmark, Sweden, and Norway have developed sailing ships capable of long-distance sea crossings.

✦ **793**
A band of raiders sails to England and attacks Lindisfarne — the first recorded raid by Vikings.

✦ **795**
The first Viking raids on Scotland and Ireland.

✦ **799**
Vikings attack France.

✦ **800s**
The main period of large, expensive ship burials.

✦ **840s**
Vikings begin to set up trading towns on the coast of Ireland.

✦ **845**
Charles the Bald, king of the French, bribes a fleet of Danish raiders with silver to persuade it to leave Paris in peace.

✦ **850-920s**
The ferocity of Viking attacks on northwest Europe is at its height.

✦ **859-862**
A fleet led by Hastein and Bjorn Ironside raids the coasts of France, Spain, North Africa, and Italy.

✦ **860**
A fleet of Swedish Vikings raids Constantinople.

✦ **865**
The Great Army, a huge horde of Danish Vikings, invades England.

✦ **About 870**
Vikings start to settle in western Iceland.

✦ **876-80**
The Great Army settles in eastern England.

✦ **886**
King Alfred of England makes peace with the settlers. Their area is called the Danelaw.

✦ **907**
Vikings in Russia draw up a trade treaty with Constantinople.

✦ **911**
Vikings start to settle in northern France.

✦ **930**
The first Althing is held in Iceland, at Thingvellir.

✦ **About 965**
The king of Denmark, Harald Bluetooth, decides to become a Christian. The rest of his country soon does the same.

✦ **About 982**
Erik the Red discovers Greenland.

✦ **1000**
Leif Eriksson sets foot on Vinland, in North America.

Icelanders at the Althing decide that their country will become Christian.

✦ **1013**
The king of Denmark, Svein Forkbeard, invades and conquers England.

✦ **1018**
Svein's son Cnut becomes king of England. He later rules Denmark, Norway, and part of Sweden.

✦ **About 1030**
Norway slowly becomes a Christian country.

✦ **1066**
King Harald Hardrada of Norway is defeated by the English at the Battle of Stamford Bridge. This is the last major Viking invasion of any of their European neighbors.

✦ **1069-70**
Svein Estrithsson, king of Denmark, makes minor raids on England, but soon makes peace.

✦ **About 1100**
Sweden finally becomes a Christian country. All the Viking lands are now Christian and have close ties with neighboring European countries. The Viking Age is over.

Author: Rachel Wright
Consultant:
   Dr. Richard Hall,
   York Archaeological
   Trust
Editors:
   Lesley Ann Daniels
   Jonathan Stroud
Designers:
   Jonathan Hair
   Louise Jackson

**Advertisement
illustrations by:**
Maxine Hamil: 26bl,
   27br, 29bl
Michaela Stewart: 15bl,
   20tr, 26br, 30bl, 30br,
   31bl
Ian Thompson: 29br, 30t,
   31ml
Peter Visscher: 23bl, 26bm
Mike White: 19bm, 20mr,
   23tl, 27bl

**Decorative borders and
small illustrations by:**
Vanessa Card: 8br
Caroline Church: 7b
Maxine Hamil: 1, 10bl,
   11bm, 13tr, 13br,
   15m, 24bl, 24br, 31
Michaela Stewart: 11br,
   11tr, 25b
Ian Thompson: 12, 20bl

With thanks to:
Artist Partners,
B. L. Kearley,
Illustration Ltd.,
Temple Rogers,
Virgil Pomfret Agency

ABOUT THE WORD "VIKING"

The people who lived in Norway, Denmark, and Sweden between 793 and 1066 were usually ruled by different kings and often fought one another. But their languages and customs had much in common, and they shared the same love of adventure.

These people did not call themselves Vikings, but a man who went looting overseas was called *víkingr*, which means "a raider." And because it was these very raids that made them famous, the word "Viking" is now used for all the people who lived in these countries during this time.

The place-names used in this book are modern ones, such as Russia or Germany. The Vikings would often have used different names.